D0673971

THE DIARY OF
EDWARD THE HAMSTER
1990–1990

Translated from the original Hamster
by Miriam Elia and Ezra Elia

B⬛XTREE

First published 2012 by Boxtree
an imprint of Pan Macmillan, a division of Macmillan Publishers Limited
Pan Macmillan, 20 New Wharf Road, London N1 9RR
Basingstoke and Oxford
Associated companies throughout the world
www.panmacmillan.com

ISBN 978-0-7522-2803-7

A CIP catalogue record for this book is available from
the British Library.

Printed and bound in China

Visit **www.panmacmillan.com** to read more about all our books
and to buy them. You will also find features, author interviews and
news of any author events, and you can sign up for e-newsletters
so that you're always first to hear about our new releases.

Preface

In the summer of 2008 I happened across just another garage sale in a leafy north London suburb.

It seemed much like any other garage sale, until I noticed the glint of a small cage flicker from under a desk. I can't say why I was drawn to it, but having opened its side door my eyes immediately alighted on a tiny document, so small I could barely read its title. I could only decipher the word 'Edward' in scrawled handwriting.

This was no ordinary discovery.

It soon transpired that the document I held in my hand would transform contemporary literature in both the human and rodent worlds. I had discovered the diary of Edward the Hamster.

It is an extraordinary work: profound meditations on the nature of captivity and the soul, interlaced with stark reflections on the grinding banalities of everyday living, illuminate its tiny pages. Edward unpicks the very fabric of tedium and forces us to question the drive that leads any of us to first take inky straw to paper. His short life is here set down in its entirety, yet his voice will surely echo through centuries to come. If you should take the time to read this intense but intimate journal, you may come to realize that Edward is not just a hamster; he is a state of mind.

Doctor M.E. Rodentstein, Specialist in Hamster Linguistics
and Philosophy at the University of Mousachusetts, 2012

THE DIARY OF
EDWARD THE HAMSTER
1990–1990

Wednesday, April 30th

It's my anniversary and no one seems to have noticed. Six months today. Six months since they 'bought' me from *Sniffles Pet Shop*.

Saturday, May 3rd

I've decided not to use the wheel again.

Sunday, May 4th

I've decided to use the wheel, but only at night, when they're sleeping. I'll scratch and crawl and rattle the cage, just to annoy them, to show them I will not do tricks – that if I do anything, it is for *me*, not for them.

The smaller one came for me today and tried to pick me up, but I ran and hid in the hay. She soon stopped.

Monday, May 5th

Why exist?

Wednesday, May 7th

Two of them came today, dragged me out of the cage and put me in some kind of improvised maze made out of books and old toilet rolls. A labyrinth with no escape. They were treating it like a game, laughing and squealing as I desperately scrabbled from blind alley to blind alley – but I knew it was no game. They're trying to crush my will, to grind me down. They can take my freedom, but they will never take my soul.

My name is Edward, and *I am a hamster*.

Thursday, May 8th

The vet came today. He touched me. Apparently, I'm a woman.

Friday, May 9th

Not a woman. I have checked.

Saturday, May 10th

Here I have everything I need. There is no reason to be unhappy.

Wednesday, May 14th

Reflections on a wheel:

> It goes around.
> It has no purpose.
> It squeaks.
> *I shall use it no longer.*

Friday, May 16th

Used the wheel.

Ate seeds. Drank water.

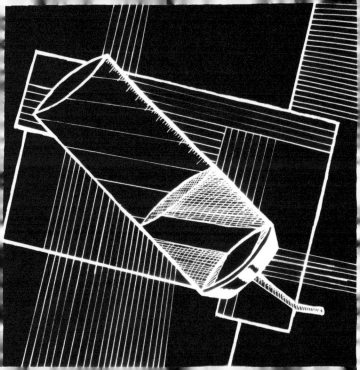

Saturday, May 17th

Today I drank my water first, and then ate the seeds.

Sunday, June 1st

Wheel

Seeds

Water.

Wheel

Seeds

Water.

IS THERE NOTHING ELSE?!

Now I take a stand. For my own rights, and for all those that suffer under the yoke of tyranny; a strike against the cruel hands of my brutal overlords.

Know that from now on I shall take no food or water till freedom . . . or death.

2.33 p.m.

Two minutes into hunger strike. I am strong and determined.

2.36 p.m.

Five minutes now. Beginning to feel weak.

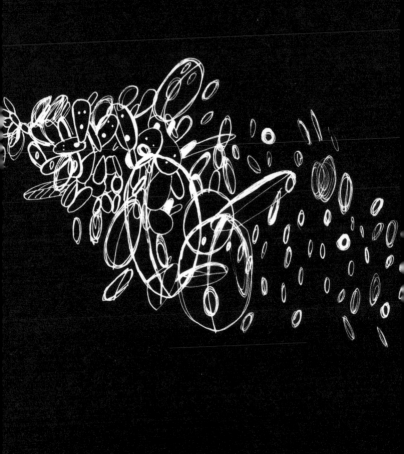

2.41 p.m. The seeds. They are taunting me!

2.45 p.m.
I have lost a gram. Maybe more.

2.47 p.m.
That is enough sacrifice for one day. What use is a dead hamster to the Resistance? So I have eaten fifty seeds and drunk my fill of water.

2.48 p.m.
POISONED! POISONED! Death stares me in the eye!

4.00 p.m.

Recovering from mild indigestion. It has been a long day.

Friday, August 1st

Today, the cat approached.

I thought it meant me harm at first – it is so very large – and it took me some time to pluck up the courage to speak, but when I did so he drew closer, as if curious to hear.

'My name is Edward! I am a hamster!' I shouted. 'Are you familiar with my species?'

He made no response, excepting a dim purr. I could make out no words.

Perhaps he was shy. If that were so, I was anxious to set him at ease, so I sought a common bond.

'Do you have a wheel?' I asked.

Again the faint purr.

My patience is small. Perhaps foolishly, I then abandoned tact.

'I see you sometimes, curled up on the window sill for hours and hours – tell me, are you drugged?'

No words again, though the low purr now broke into a distinct 'meow'. Gathering confidence, I elected to speak plainly.

'I believe in freedom, you see – for all furry animals, large or small. I know that we are of different species, but you and I – we are both part of a system. And that system must be broken.'

A kernel of an idea began to form in my mind.

'If we came together, we could throw off the shackles of our oppression – I as the head, you as the fist. Nothing could stand in our way!'

The idea was so beautiful that I stood shivering under the weight of its simple power for a few short moments.

The cat uttered another meow, and peering into its round, grey eyes, I realized the truth.

He is just a dumb and senseless brute – he is allowed to roam free, for the bars are locked firm on his mind.

Monday, August 4th

They came for me today – I thought for a moment they would set me free – deluded fool. They placed me on the ground, but something was wrong.

I was at once in the world and separated from it . . . by some manner of force field – *an invisible ball* – providing only an illusion of the freedom I have craved so long.

Why do they taunt me so?

Wednesday, August 20th

The ball again. This time I was ready. As before, I was whisked from the cage and violently thrust inside. My heart pounded, yet I remained still as a rock and watched until I saw their attention had drifted.

Then I sprang for the open door, straining with every sinew, every muscle, every fibre of my being, moving faster and faster till I had built an unstoppable momentum toward that long corridor of light, that opened and yawned before me as I drew closer – and closer . . .

A foot suddenly blocked my path and pushed me away from freedom. I fell back, a defeated and broken hamster.

They are playful in their cruelty.

Wednesday, September 3rd

Why write? Life is a cage of empty words.

Wednesday, September 10th

Eight months old today. Oh, the things I've seen.

The Wheel.
The Tray.
The Ball.
The Whe— no, I forget.

Thursday, September 11th

I must fight this lethargy. My pen grows heavy. The seed box
beckons . . . the hay . . .

Saturday, September 20th

They opened the cage door today. And left it open for five
. . . ten minutes. I stared at the open space, cowering under
the hay, wanting to go but *terrified* of leaving. Why didn't I
escape?! Isn't that all I want? Freedom? The freedom to
make my own way, to . . .

. . . something is moving. I can see it now. Perhaps it's the
wind...? No – there is no wind here.

At last! A comrade!

A hamster also, I think. He appears tired. He sleeps now.

Am feverish with excitement.

Sunday, September 21st

And still he sleeps. I can barely contain myself in anticipation of a true intellectual dialogue. Oh, how I have craved this moment!

I wonder what he is? A thinker, perhaps. A *philosophe*?

Or perhaps a maker of things, whose very craft has led him to contemplate truth, life and the nature of our captivity. Perhaps he has found a compromise. He seems content.

I will rest a while to gather myself for our first *entente*.

Monday, September 22nd

He is awake. Tried to engage him in conversation for a moment but he seemed groggy. Understandable after such a long sleep.

Now he eats in the corner. He makes quite a noise.

Tuesday, September 23rd

He uses the wheel. He is yet to show any interest in me. Perhaps he needs to stimulate himself first with exercise.

Wednesday, September 24th

He is still on the wheel. Beginning to sense that he is toying with me.

Thursday, September 25th

He eats again.

When will he dispense with this infernal charade?!

I will confront him at first light.

Friday, September 26th

He says his name is Wolf, although he is not a wolf.

He is a hamster.

I tried to goad him into debate on the nature of our captivity, on the emptiness of life and our irrational will to live.

He burped, laughed and defecated in the food tray.

He is either mad, or profoundly stupid.

I am crushed.

He sleeps again. Perhaps I shall do the same.

It is my only option.

Sunday, September 28th

His vacuous enthusiasm for life is driving me to distraction.
On he bustles – now eating, now sleeping. To what end?
What is his legacy? What might others learn from him?

I must sleep. He takes to the wheel again.

Monday, September 29th

That infernal noise is driving me *insane*. Four hours of this – pointless scrabbling and squeaking – *round and round* it goes. Still, if I'm not sleeping, then neither are those that keep me here, in this cage. Where are they? In bed, curled up in a ball? Head under a pillow? Watching something on television, perhaps? Or maybe they're sat up, eyes reddened, staring at the cold, empty pages of a diary like mine, scribbling across it, line after line after line of anguished, meaningless rubbish, all to the deafening squeaking and scrabbling of that *bastard* wheel–!

Tuesday, September 30th

It wouldn't take much to kill him – would it? . . . I don't think I have the strength to wring his neck in cold blood . . . All that work on the wheel has made him physically stronger than someone . . . more *reflective* like me.

And yet perhaps I could use his cherished wheel against him . . . I'll loosen the screws so that next time – tomorrow, when he's awake, he'll climb up and come crashing down, crushed beneath the weight of that monstrous circle of death. He'll squeal for help but I'll watch him writhe and then perhaps . . . perhaps I'll be able to sleep.

Wednesday, October 1st

He sleeps.

Loosened screws.

Thursday, October 2nd

My plan is no closer to fruition. He gets up . . . eats . . . rests
again . . . and still the wheel sits undisturbed . . . He knows
something . . . How is he able to gobble so much for so long,
and make *so much noise*?

Twenty-five hours and no sleep. Delirious . . . the cage bars
bend themselves into long rows of shiny teeth – they chatter,
part, close and part – I hear a voice but can discern no words.

It is not a voice, but a gnashing, gargling sound.

My God! It is him!

He is choking!

Watched him struggle for a last shallow breath.

Poor wretch. I felt a twinge of pity.

Saturday, October 4th

Strange day. They were quite excited when they found him. The larger one put his hand in the cage and removed the body while the others made peculiar squealing noises . . . as if they were actually enjoying it . . . though I couldn't be sure. They let me be, anyhow.

Funny: I feel all the more alone, now. Not that Wolf offered any meaningful conversation. Only that I would enjoy some stimulating company. I shouldn't weaken myself with any vain hopes, however.

I know that I am destined to live, and die, alone.

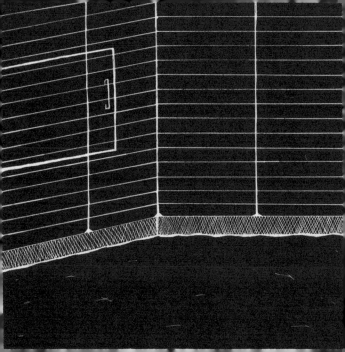

Wednesday, October 15th

Death is the final cage.

None shall escape.

Sunday, October 19th

I write, but what do words amount to? A few scratches on a bald, white surface. I have lost the urge to record.

Nothing is of any consequence.

Tuesday, October 21st

Something has arrived; I think another hamster.

I will not raise my hopes this time.

Wednesday, October 22nd

It is a she. She approaches now.

Her name is Camilla.

Thursday, October 23rd

At last! Dialogue!

She terms herself an artist. She makes compositions to reflect her thoughts and feelings. Her medium is hay. In her words, what she makes today, she may destroy tomorrow – such is the ephemeral nature of being.

I struggle to disagree.

Friday, October 24th

Read Camilla extracts from this diary. She wept, but said nothing.

Saturday, October 25th

Made love.

Sunday, October 26th

Stole a glance at Camilla's journal while she slept. Here is what I read:

'Wasting away in a miserable cage at the back of another pet shop, one day I caught my reflection in the water bowl and I thought, "Camilla, *why give up*? Do something, *make* something – *anything* to keep this dreadful loneliness from consuming you alive . . ." Since then, I have devoted every spare waking moment to my compositions . . . to continuously re-creating myself through work. For even though we are trapped behind these terrible bars, our minds – our souls – are free as *art*, which is limitless.'

Is this love?

Monday, October 27th

Our connection transcends language.

I am complete.

I watch her fall asleep. She has warned me she grows restless at night. I look forward to her stirrings.

Tuesday, October 28th

Awoken by a terrible snap and crash. The wheel is askew.
Beneath it lies Camilla. Her body is cold.

Wednesday, October 29th

They fixed the wheel today. I've decided never to use it again.

It stands as a monument to my beloved.

Saturday, November 1st

Unbearable emptiness. Cannot write.

Without love there is no hope.

Sunday, November 2nd

Terrible pain.

I know that I am lucky to have spent only a few short hours with Camilla. She may be gone, but she has left me the greatest gift any hamster could receive:

Truth.

Thursday, November 6th

An answer to my prayers: the cage door is ajar. Today I journey into the vast unknown. Camilla's star will guide me.

I must re-invent myself and start afresh. I leave this diary behind.

Friday, November 7th

I have returned.

Is this cage of my own making?

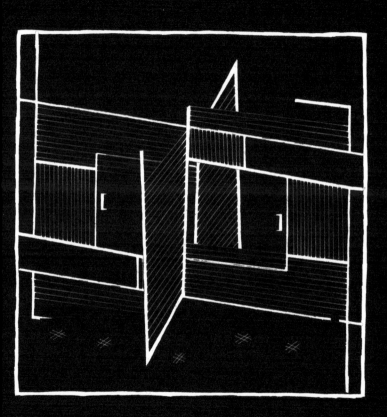

Monday, November 10th

What is real?

I eat, but I cannot taste.

I think, but I do not feel.

I write, but I do not understand. My dreams are vivid.
Life – less so.

A blurred hand snakes into my cage. It is a venomous, sneaky thing – the instrument of my suffering. I shall take no more of this – I shall strike against it.

I shall bite!

The blood draws easily. A piercing scream! I am thrown to the cage floor. There, I lie still.

I do not know what fate awaits me, though I am sure it shall bring an end.

Tuesday, November 11th

The cage moves. I am cast into darkness. When the light returns, it is different and colder . . . The walls around shine white and sterile.

Gloved hands pry about the cage. A masked face hovers above. It is like the sun.

My name is Edward, and I am a hamster.

I pass into shadow, though this diary may carry a part of me into eternal light.

A Note on the Authors

Miriam Elia and her brother, Ezra Elia, were once the proud owners of an unusually gloomy hamster called Edward. He died some time ago, but left an enduring mark on their collective psyche, as he is the only living being either of them has ever attempted to take care of. Since his death, both Miriam and Ezra have become excessively selfish and miserable, and they now lead a cloistered life, in silence only disturbed by the pen scratchings of each other's writing and drawing.